SOUTH AFRICA READY FOR A ONE PARTY STATE

First published (précis) 2016

Published by Letlhage Raphuti

Tel: +27 (0) 11 973 0023

Mobile: +27 (0) 82 643 5911

email: letlhage@tlhagets.com

P.O. Box 12351, Benoryn, 1504, Gauteng, South Africa.

ISBN: 978-0-620-73773-9 (Print)

ISBN: 978-0-620-73774-6 (e-pub)

ISBN: 978-0-620-73775-3 (Kindle)

SOUTH AFRICA READY FOR

A ONE PARTY STATE

Letlhage Raphuti

"As long as poverty, injustice and gross inequality persist in our world, none of us can truly rest"- Nelson Mandela

This book symbolises a journey of consciousness within and outside our surroundings. A journey that have been inspired by many people in their true convictions. It is dedicated to all of you, to you the reader, to all South Africans and all nations.

To my family. I pour my abundant gratitude.

Thank You.

Contents

Introduction

A mind-blowing reflection on the existence of the colonial state in the current dispensation. A link is found to be existing on the socio-economic landscape with the colonial state. This book touches on millions and millions of people still trapped under a colonial economic bondage, and the threat to democracy. The narrative reveal the implication of the current political, economic and electorate system on the society. Reflecting on issues that are fundamental to freedom, but at the same time found to be stubborn to eradicate. It further zooms into the inability of the system to rescue about 23 million citizens out of the existing economic bondage.

__Author__

1

Stubborn Stains of Freedom

There is a say that freedom in South Africa did not come free. Reflecting on colonial powers, human oppression, brutality against humanity, including the struggle to dismantle these evil acts. Yes, it is true, freedom did not come free. It came at a cost of massive human sacrifices. However most progressive goals remain unaccomplished in the struggle for total emancipation of humanity. These are stubborn stains of freedom. They include, land ownership and transfer back to indigenous people, economic freedom, the economy is still in the hands of the minority group regardless of Blacks being over 80% majority in the land.

Agriculture is still in the hands of whites, who are not the vanguards of food security for the majority population. Black people are still poor in their wealthy country. Over quarter of the population (8 million) is unemployed, majority being young people. A lot of gains have been made by democracy, however only in some parts. This is not enough considering the amount of time a democracy was installed. No one can ever be free as long as millions of people still live in shacks, millions still stand in very long queues the whole day in health facilities to receive basic health care, crime increase in communities and millions are wondering where their next meal will come from.

Is this a political problem? a social problem? an economic problem? It is a combination of all. Then if it is a political problem, why do we have this problem post-apartheid era. One can only imagine that the unveiling of democracy did not address to the core the underlying socio-economic issues. Blacks did not suffer and die in struggle to continue to be poor. It has all been talks that equality should be accomplished, socially and economically.

The truth is colonial beneficiaries are refusing to cooperate. Transformation is not happening as it should.

Each year the Employment Equity Report gives shocking findings. The mining sector, regardless of existing interventions such as mining charters, refuses to transform and implement these interventions. A typical white monopoly capital behaviour that insist on the exclusion of Black People from the main stream. Manufacturing and other sectors are behaving the same.

Black Economic Empowerment have not addressed these challenges. Only a handful Blacks can be accounted. The nation cannot celebrate this in the face of millions of South Africans still going to bed hungry. Why are there no consequences on these sectors if they fail to implement targets? White monopoly capital still gets away with this pattern behavior, which is anti-black empowerment.

The revolution is popular with songs such as " Senzeni na, Senzeni na, Senzeni na, Senzeni na, Senzeni na, Senzeni na, Senzeni na, Senzeni na" the nation is still asking the very same question, Senzeni na? Whites talk everything like crime, corruption, social immorality, but wouldn't dare talk about equality, land redistribution, poverty, improvement of the lives of Blacks, relinquishing minerals. Why? Because the nation remain a divided nation and whites still believe in white supremacy and black slavery.

They attack everything
that the democratic
government is doing but
would not dare speak
about trillions of rands
that are being stolen from
Black nations

They attack everything that the democratic government is doing but would not dare speak about trillions of rands that are being stolen from Black nations. They will not talk about racism that still prevail in our boundaries, they will not talk about industry captains receiving exorbitant payouts from their corrupt economic activities. They will not talk about company collisions, price fixing, transfer pricing, tax evasions, but will go on to talk about corruption in government and Black companies. This is not a suggestion that there is no corruption in government, but a mere pointing out the stereotype behavior of those who continue to see Blacks as terrorists, criminals, inferior beings and objects.

This imbalance of believe points to an unreconciled society. South Africa have become a nation where Blacks are the ones who reach out to reconciliation, but unfortunately whites do not do the same. Wealth redistribution is not an option, it is a must. The nation has said they want to see this happen, whites have not said we will do our part and make it happen.

One thing that comes to mind is that the 1994 dispensation was not adequate. Blacks know that it is up to them to define their destiny. Nothing should force them anymore to remain subject of the colonial trade systems, colonial financial systems, colonial agricultural systems. Majority of people with their resources should define their food security, decide how, when, with whom to trade. Decide on their use of land. It cannot be right that till 22 years of democracy, 79% of land is still in white hands. Again, all the time that this issue is raised, white economists counter this reality with a notion that post 1994, majority of land have been allocated to blacks. Justifying this notion with portions of land allocated for RDP houses and totally neglecting the economic side of land.

With that being said, what is the cause of land invasions? Majority of land is still in the hands of minority people. So, you still have the land issue that fails to resolve, while on the other side, poverty striking the Black Population. On the other side having pockets of whites justifying the status quo to be correct and just.

Perhaps let us take a moment to reflect. What is the impact of 1994 democracy and its declaration. What would have been the impact of a different dispensation?

1994 democracy and its declaration

Government of National Unity

Reconciliation

Reconstruction and Development

Alternative dispensation

Nationalisation of mines, banks,etc)

Revamp of commercial sectors

Restructure the economy to absorb the majority population

Establish new bi-literal trade terms

Own currency on minerals and other resources

Disband all colonial trade systems

The 1994 dispensation has its own mega successes. However, the dispensation continues to carry millions of the population in poverty, unemployment and inequalities. It cannot be concluded that it has sufficiently served the souls of many who perished and suffered during the colonial system. Until justice is achieved in these areas, where majority of the population live in prosperity, Project Reconstruction and Development remain partly achieved.

It is mentioned that this project was crucial as it avoided potential conflict which could have led to many civilian deaths. The truth is, many still lost their lives in the process and the nation was divided.

Whether double, triple or more conflict could have been encountered if an alternative declaration was applied.

The question would be, who would be fighting who? What would be the forces? The bottom line is that the oppressed would still be the same person and that the proportion would not have changed. The oppressed had already prepared itself for force as it embarked on an armed struggle. Digging holes in community streets where armored military vehicles got trapped and the community striking back at military forces was part of already existing struggle.

Blacks had already been killed by white forces.

Many and thousands had died. Death had already been part of the struggle. Week after week communities burying numbers of community members, brutally shot by white forces. Nights before days of burials, night vigils would be held to celebrate their lives and comfort the families. These were peaceful gatherings.

White soldiers would budge in, start arresting and shooting innocent civilians. It therefore cannot be correct to suggest that a different dispensation could have caused civil deaths. The war had already been in motion. A course of reconciliation was adopted as part of CODESA project to facilitate transition into democracy in favour of an armed struggle. A move said to have not been supported by all in the liberation circles.

Of Course, the process was preceded by liberation movement leaders and other political prisoners being released from prison and the unbanning of the liberation parties.

This must be acknowledged as it was a gigantic accomplishment for the nation. I guess careful political moves and compromises had to be made. The question is, what have been compromised and why? The forces against the apartheid government, even without having applied

It is just not impossible to uplift the livelihood of majority of our beloved population. The political system in our country have reduced the lives of its civilians to political parties the armed struggle had already made its in rows. This force could still have been applied to facilitate the release of political prisoners and unbanning the liberation parties.

The force could again still be applied to adopt an alternative declaration. The force was enough to reclaim land from unlawful owners, redistribute wealth and adopt a constitution to this effect. You cannot be a beggar in your own home.

In fact, this is what the masses of this country had voted for. In a burning society of ours to still achieve economic freedom, it would be sensible to institute a referendum on key economic issues. It is said the ruling party does not have enough majority to change the constitution. Maybe not, but the nation has the power to decide democratically on the direction of their livelihood. This is not the only societal machinery available but there are others.

It is just not impossible to uplift the livelihood of majority of our beloved population. The political system in our country have reduced the lives of its civilians to political parties. Media is failing significantly to project a good course of the society. Its agenda have been drawn to winners and losers of political parties and neglecting the core existence of the nation. White capital monopoly operates sideways to democratic and development agenda. Alternative approaches are required to remove the stubborn stains of freedom.

2

War against humanity

Africa, the south lowermost is a landscape rich with mineral deposits under, above and around its surface. Its inhabitants survived adequately and peacefully on these shores. They discovered its provisions for living. A human evolution that took place peacefully. Only to be disturbed by uninvited white dutch and portuguese who invaded the area for selfish, criminal and brutal reasons.

They found physical deposits of minerals in the hands of its inhabitants. That is how they discovered availability of such minerals, and launched a massive exploration. It is not true that white people discovered these minerals. They were looking for something that was already discovered by the land inhabitants.

They then illegally and forcefully claimed ownership of the land. An act that disturbed peace in the land and took away natural evolution of its inhabitants. Over 340 years, South Africa was colonized by these brigands. White people, settlers. This barbarism installed an act of injustice and brutality against Africans in their native land in the south. This was not an isolated and unique practice, but one that saw many African countries going through the same surgical procedure.

Land and its natural resources was forcefully and unlawfully dispossessed from inhabitants of the land for nothing but inhumane and criminal reasons. This was a crime of theft, brutality and murder by whites to force their settlement in a foreign land.

Done so because the country and its continent is bestowed with rich minerals, and whites applied a brutal theft machinery to steal from the land. Taking unlawful ownership and turning peaceful native inhabitants into slaves. Everything was priced including human souls. Inhabitants disgustingly sold and bought at a price.

An act that disturbed peace
in the land and took away
natural evolution of its
inhabitants.

A living soul on the land turned into a commodity for slavery.

Oppression against Africans took its unbearable shape and later apartheid system that meant Black People were not human to be in the same space as whites. A system that meant that the only human beings on the land were white people. During this period, Black People suffered so much pain. A natural feeling of affirmation that Blacks are living beings and not as defined by whites. A defined act of removing dignity and pride from the Blacks Nation. An act that was inhumanely institutionalised and lagalised. When you strip dignity out of a human being, you kill that being.

Military machinery was installed to ensure that security is preserved to keep order in a criminal installed system, and to ensure that theft of wealth is protected.

Whites put themselves above everything, proclaimed supremacy and declared wisdom that they know everything. They did not, they never knew the power of pain and what it can manifest into. Resistance to this pain emerged to reject inhumanity and injustice instilled in the people of the land. Resistance against segregation, pass laws, inequalities, and many other political and socio-economic systems that decoded Blacks inferior and slaves to whites. History and archives account for hundreds and thousands of these practices.

Countless of innocent Black people died being innocently shot and tortured by white people. Many families lost their loved ones and many still don't know where to find the remains of their loved ones. A pain that continue to strike many families. Thousands and thousands were jailed for many years in prison and classified as terrorists. Lost time to spend with their families and raise their children.

Many others, young and old were forced to escape living in their native land. This was a very painful period that saw a Black Person not only loose his humanity, but also the ability to nature a **GIFT** to live out of provided natural resources.

During this period whites installed colonial systems of governance and trade to rob Africa of its resources. While land was forcefully removed from the hands of Black People, whites indulged in exploitation of mineral and natural resources. Livestock, crops, diamonds, gold, iron ore, platinum, land military fell in the hands of whites. They claimed ownership of agriculture and mining on a Black Person land.

This was a very painful period that saw a Black Person not only loose his humanity, but also the ability to nature a **GIFT** to live out of provided natural resources.

Colonial trade commenced with Blacks being captured as slaves and traded for pieces of shillings to other whites who needed labour to farm and exploit the land. A Black Person became nothing but an object to dig grounds to extract diamonds, gold and other minerals, an object to scrub a white person floor, an object to do all sort of labour a white person sought to do. Whites crafted laws to allow and legitimise this evil practice.

No Black Person was allowed to partake in commercial activities and advance a life of a Black Person.

An Apartheid system was instilled to separate a Black Person from human evolution. Under this system Blacks were not allowed to share toilets, shops, beaches, workplaces with whites. Blacks were again forcefully removed from their land, when whites earmarked those areas for commercial and white settlements.

In a course to reverse these evil white practices, Blacks organised themselves in structural formations, movements and political parties. A killed soul transforming into a re-born black strength. A natural firebrand gift that no human being, race or any form of machinery can take away. The Black organisation was born to dismantle war against humanity. It was aimed at reversing white supremacy and oppression against the nation. Organisation took place within communities and developed ideologies to counter the unjust practices. They grew by the day as hundreds and thousands of people joined to form the revolution on the South African soil and in solidarity with the African continent struggle. Schools, universities, places of work, community centers turned into mobilising grounds. These brave and selfless initiatives saw its success in many ways. Growth in the formation of the united Black front, increase in the number of activists, creation of the new culture of black participation, solidarity in many parts of the continent and the world.

Ultimately and ground breaking the dismantle of the apartheid government and installation of the Democratic Government. However the dismantle of apartheid government does not mean that the apartheid system and imperialism has collapsed altogether.

Why say so? Twenty two years after the fall of apartheid government, Blacks reflect and ask themselves some of these questions.

Did formations achieve what they aimed for?

Are we liberated?

Are we free?

Are we still slaves?

Did we attain back the land?

Did we obtain back the livestock?

Did we acquire back minerals?

Did we claim back the economy?

Did we implant back our humanity?

These questions are burning in the scape of our land and can be summed up as, yes blacks obtained freedom but only part of it. Therefore, liberation achieved only part of its objective. Most of the liberation goals have not been accomplished.

3

An Enemy of Democracy

Unemployment in South Africa is a colossal problem. A landmark of untransformed and snail pace developing society. Shockingly enough is that the nation is amongst the top 15 worst unemployment rate countries in the world. The nation is ranked top 10 in Africa and within 10 and 15 in the world. The rate of unemployment persists above 25% year on year. Although the standing has demonstrated a roller coaster pattern between year 2000 and 2016, hitting an all high of 31% in 2003 and a lowest mark of 21% in 2008. An average rate until 2016 is 25% mark. This represent a 6-8 million people without jobs.

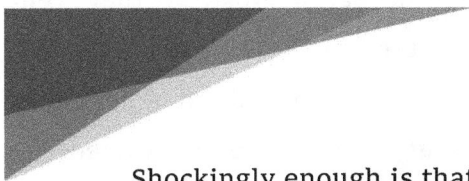

Shockingly enough is that the nation is amongst the top 15 worst unemployment rate countries in the world

It also presents a significant proportion of people, in the region of 2.5 million persons who are discouraged to find any work. Most have stopped looking due to loss of hope.

The socio-economic scenario has remained unbearably catastrophic in a democratic phase. A phase supposed to be a period of hope. A period wherein millions stood up in rainy cold sunny days to reinstall dignity in their lives through a ballot. Instead they remain in shattered conditions for years after years.

In those years, they continue to be joined by many others who without choice are instructed by their employers to exit their employ. How does a nation fall in this category being the economic leader in the continent? Regardless of policy interventions being developed and put in place, the problem continues to grow.

Let us pause for a moment and reflect on what may be fair or unfair comparison. In 2016 South Africa have a population of above 55million. America has a population of 324 million and United Kingdom have 65million population.

Theoretically South Africa is 6 times population smaller to the US and relatively next to equal to the population of the United Kingdom. While we pause, let us forget a bit about definitions of these states as either developed or underdeveloped or emerging countries. The bottom line is that all are living human beings who all have the same basic and natural living needs. Interestingly US with its large population have an unemployment rate at 4.8%. The U.K is standing at the same rate of unemployment, being 4.9%.

Of course, the economic characteristics of these economies differ and perform differently.

However, whatever the differences are, it is evident regardless of a huge different size of population that the economies of the UK and the US absorb a significant rate of the population into the job market. Something that the South African economic model fails dismally to achieve. For this purpose, let us not enter into depth technical analysis but rather focus on what all political formations are using as a promise to the people. They all promise job creation. The question is how does a small population with all its minerals, wealth and vast land, fail to absorb the population into the labour market. Is the country having a society that does not want to work? Do industries not create enough employment? Is it a responsibility of the state to create employment? Is the economy structured to best serve the big giants? Well whatever the answer to these questions is, the fact is millions of people continue to be unemployed and earn no income. So, going back to earlier citation, they cannot afford to get basic and natural needs that every human being require. Poverty continue to strike in these circumstances.

Further to this is the core fundamentals of human development. An evolution from childhood to adulthood. A basic reality of being in school at a particular age and entering an employment phase at a particular age. A requisite to start a family, have children and the list goes on and on and on.

A basic need for shelter and food remain a living right through this stages. Does a nation have a higher birth rate compared to the economic growth rate? Have labour market reached its labour absorption ceiling? The reality is that the inequality gap between the rich and poor continues to widen. Parallel to this is the fact that the unemployment space is also capturing millions of Black graduates.

This is at the backdrop of a capitalist system which continue to drive huge profits at the expense of the poor society. While profits in industries are growing substantially, expansion programmes are not in place to absorb more people into the labour market.

It has become the CEO's mission to drive industries to maximize investors wealth more than to drive profits. A very interesting phenomenon of capitalism

Investors pull out of companies that bend to workers demands. When new investors come on board, they come with conditions for reducing labour costs

Captains of the industry enjoy huge benefits and bonuses for growing profits, while majority of people remain unemployed.

Well another side to this is wealth accumulation. It has become the CEO's mission to drive industries to maximize investors wealth more than to drive profits. A very interesting phenomenon of capitalism. Adding to this phenomenon is the existence of labour unions and their strive for better working conditions and wages. It is found in many instances that companies who ultimately bend to wage demands and better worker's conditions, ultimately retrench workers over time. This also contribute substantially to high levels of unemployment. Investors pull out of companies that bend to workers demands. When new investors come on board, they come with conditions for reducing labour costs. This result in many losing their jobs and contributing to high unemployment rate.

Capitalism continue to cripple the societal development and the mindset between capitalism and socialism is far from reaching an equilibrium. The gap is much wide between the rich and the poor. This present a societal dilemma that creates a non-harmonised environment.

A great philosopher articulates that a poor person living next to a rich person suffers great displeasure than a poor person with no rich person next to him. It cannot be correct that a nation rich in minerals, manufacturing and land cannot absorb its marginalised population into the labour system. This continue to happen in a land of majority black people, and majority of unemployed people are blacks. Dominated by youth, a future generation. The economic model in existence is not structured correctly.

Trillions of rands made in commercial activities should be diverted to job creation programmes by the private sector. The private sector should set responsive job creation targets within a short period of time to turn around the situation and commit to implementing these programmes. Time should pass where only government set this agenda and fails to achieve it, as a result of the private sector not responding. In the non-response, the private sector is still not held to account and there are no consequences.

Foreign investments should not be implemented at the expense of employing only 1 or two black people year on year. They should come with massive job creation programmes which have long term socio-economic impact.

Government usually announces multi-billion rand projects to be implemented over time. Budgets are passed and spent on multi-national companies who enjoy huge profits out of these projects. One cannot help to say, these does not justify the unemployment in society. Another form of colonialism where majority of blacks remain poor and government funding is used to enrich multi-national companies. I shall not touch on the slow economic growth at this point, cause the high unemployment rate contribute to this.

Another aspect of this epidemic is price transfer, tax evasions, collisions, by the evil capitalism behaviour. Billions of rands leave the country unaccounted. These monies if reserved properly can be channelled through employment programmes. Despite all these challenges and illegal behaviour, it can be seen that Blacks are still regarded as mere objects in this country by whites. Nothing much have changed from a colonial system. This is an enemy to democracy and should be defeated at all cost. A programme for wealth redistribution and empowerment of the nation cannot be undermined.

4

One Party State

One cannot help but to remanence on the impact and effectiveness of an inclusive party state on the nation. In a new democratic state. A state within which a variety of political parties are ostensibly assuming representation through an electoral system. Having zoomed at the state of affairs on a political landscape.

Too much was happening at around times. Not to say nothing ever happens at any time in any political space. There is at all times controversy, fight over ideology, opposition politics, nation outcry over services, corruption, international affairs and so on. In all these, one can only imagine that the energy imbued in the nation was nothing but too negative and the danger was that it was divisive of the nation.

1994 dispensation installed a government of national unity which had a representation of various political parties. This was necessary as a core pillar to transition, transformation, nation building and healing. The electoral system carried this system through the subsequent years in a democratic state. However, with its good intentions, politics shifted so much from nation building at the society level to politics at political party level. Forces became strong that political parties emerged as flamboyant competitors of a political space. The ruling party was getting divided on its own. Weaknesses stained the party and reflections of these are in government.

Corruption and many other weaknesses in governance became an order of the day. Forces from the opposition found an opportunity for grandstanding and attacking the ruling party. Well it is said that it is the job of the opposition. A practice seen as normal and opportunistic.

New battle lines got drawn between parties and enemy bases formed. I guess this is politics in its nature. However, one can ask, does this serve the nation in a

The electoral system carried
this system through the
subsequent years in a
democratic state. However,
with its good intentions,
politics shifted so much from
nation building at the society
level to politics at political
party level

positive way? Is it healthy in a new democratic state? When these fights are fought between political parties, where is the nation? Nothing featured in the agenda that represented people of the country. These fights are fought over the power to govern and millions of citizens are neglected as a result. The only time they are mentioned, is when they are used for mere politicking games. The opposition busy attacking the ruling party with a clear mission to unseat it from government and the ruling party defending itself from all forces that came blazing against it. We saw parliament degenerating into a state of unparliamentary activity. If this is not true, I plead not to be judged, this is what media projected. On the other side, media is dominated and controlled by white bourgeoisie and imperialists. They have their own crystal agenda. So, they play a pillar role on forming the perception of the nation.

The bottom line is, where are millions of citizens who continue to remain in the bottom line of the society. Who continue to remain poor, unemployed, without proper shelter, water, sanitation. Continue to receive low level of health care. They are left to sort themselves out there in the jungle.

Unemployment remain at catastrophic level. Shack dwellings are still on the rise and inter-provincial migrations continue to be the order of the day. Family formations are seriously compromised by these migrations, killing the basic moral values of society.

This environment is explosive in its nature. It is unjust, cruel and constitutionally incorrect to neglect the basic needs of the people. While it is ok for political parties to fight for dominance in the political space, it is criminal and immoral to do so at the expense of citizens. The ruling party seems not to have power. The power it requires to govern and deliver on people's mandate.

On the contrary, majority of people have given the ruling party the power to govern. Not the power to defend its political space. This environment consumes a lot of energy into unnecessary activities that are not nation building, society developmental and essential in a new democracy. A new democracy requires an around the clock dedication to implementation of peoples wishes. It requires an undivided state to deliver on this mandate.

The only feasible model suitable to this age is a One Party State. The government of national unity and inclusive state had played its role well in a transition

There is nowhere where people vote for the opposition parties to hold the ruling party to account to them. A notion fraudulently instilled as a democratic opposition role. There are institutions created by the constitution for the state to account

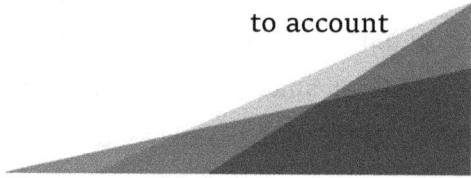

phase. However, this state model is too costly, divisive and destructive to a development phase. A One Party State looks at the state that is controlled wholly by the party installed by the majority of people. A state that should be constituted by members representing the will of the people. The elected party should focus their energy fully in serving the plight of the people, of course of all citizens.

Constitutionally people vote for what they require and they choose a party to deliver on their needs. This is the basis for voting. If this is not exercised, then injustice is practiced over the people of the country. There cannot be another way. There is nowhere where people vote for the opposition parties to hold the ruling party to account to them. A notion fraudulently instilled as a democratic opposition role. There are institutions created by the constitution for the state to account. But most importantly the governing party should account to people. People should be the baton holder of their interests.

The electoral system should be reformed to give people the power to govern. Not leave it completely to political parties.

The country needs radical electoral and legislative reform. Some may think, "wait a minute, are you suggesting what I'm thinking"? No I am not suggesting that. I'm simply saying in a democratic state, if majority of people have chosen a particular destiny and a party to deliver on that course. The party should be allowed to deliver on that course. Yes of course if it fails to do that, the electoral system should provide necessary tools to the people to change course and choose an alternative party.

Time between when those choices can be made, can be decided by the nation. For example, if elections are every five years and people feel the period is too long to leave the ruling party on its own. A shorter period can be introduced, or a referendum in between can be introduced. A referendum will play a significant role in this system. This will also allow for change in policy direction. Peoples governance should not be interfered by opposition forces. Opposition parties must fight their political battles with the ruling party in a political field. But outside government. The governing party must govern without unnecessary interference.

In this way, the elected state will spend their entire energy delivering on the will of the people. The time they currently use to defend themselves from other forces will be channeled towards delivering on people's mandate. This of course does not seek to suggest that the opposition parties should be suppressed. But opposition should contest their spaces in rightful spaces, in the opposition space.

The opposition will always oppose the ruling party objectives. In its nature insulting majority people choice of these objectives.

They use whatever state provisions to highlight their opposing position. Even when they know they stand no chance of winning their position.

There is nothing wrong with this, but opposition parties should use political spaces outside state spaces to achieve their party objectives. Disagreements always become an outcome leading to voting on a particular issue. The party with the greatest numbers usually wins the position, then losers accuse the ruling party of using its majority numbers to win their course. Wait a minute, is that not democracy? So why should there be insults about applying democratic methodology. The lust for power to rule as a minority is a dangerous and destructive desire. An evil act and desire that had previously put the nation under oppression. This should be rejected with conviction because this rule is the same as the minority rule that ruled the country over many brutal years.

The lust for power to rule as a minority is a dangerous and destructive desire. An evil act and desire that had previously put the nation under oppression. This should be rejected with conviction because this rule is the same as the minority rule that ruled the country over many brutal years

Defeated by peoples' power, the will of the people. Currently the application of democratic representation mechanism is inverse and a total waste of time and resources. While this is happening, delivery on the mandate of people is compromised. In the same breath, the incumbent state cannot falter on peoples decision of their needs, policy and legislative issues. Alteration to that cannot be effected only at the state level without involvement of the nation.

This is wrong, completely incorrect. Today the nation is held at a corner with a notion that the ruling party cannot alter the constitution because it does not have enough electoral votes to do so. Maybe yes because of the unfortunate system that is in place. But the people have the power to decide on constitutional matters and a different policy course if they so wish.

Adoption of a One Party State is the core. Addition to that is to effect the referendum system. South Africa is a new democratic state and cannot be held hostage in systems that do not work anymore. Or one that is not flexible such as to allow itself to find what works best for the people. Majority of people cannot wait helplessly another century or more to achieve required change.

Some analysis suggests that it will take more than 200 years to accomplish required land redistribution, inequality redress and adequately improve the lives of majority people. So, if systems and institutions do not work to adequately advance the lives of the people. Why wait centuries to accomplish this.

In a new maturing democracy, radical changes are required in systems that do not work. The implementation of a One Party State does not suggest or aim to marginalise the voice of the minority but it aims to radically deliver on the democratic mandate. Institutions of democracy should strongly reflect peoples power and should be instituted to represent the will of the people. If governance systems are not adequate or on time responsive, they instill danger of stagnation. An event that is costly, politically, financially, socially, economically, and one that cannot be afforded at all cost.

Streamlining governance to maximum output is the best option. The other side to this is to merge the national-provincial elections with local government elections. If the country can afford two elections in five years, then it can afford mechanisms in between, such as referendums. Why should the country have one election for national-provincial government and the other for local government? It is clear that in current system, it is difficult to separate local elections and national elections. The danger is that people vote for national issues, bread and butter issues, service delivery issues in national elections. Again, vote for national issues, bread and butter issues, service delivery issues in local government elections. Why then ask people to separate the issues? Even in election manifestos of political parties, there is no clear separation of the issues.

It is also time consuming to implement the electoral system in this way. The two-year gap of the two elections does not do justice in a new democracy. This does not serve a purposeful role. This system compound too much confusion and lead to unintended consequences. The major disbenefit to the nation is that it can bring a mixture of different political parties governing different spheres of government. This is not healthy at all. Governing power cannot be split in this way. It may look good on some political parties and bad on other political parties. The reality is that it does not serve justice to millions of citizens. This does nothing but elevate the power war between the parties. Time, energy and resources gets diverted to political power instead of needs of the people.

Unfortunately, an aching side is parties using poor people as the ticket for politicking. There is a huge, great, gigantic conflict in governance in the current three spheres of governance. National government being governed by a specific party, provincial by a different party and some municipalities governed by another party. This cannot work. Who suffers at the end? People of the country.

Who control the budget? Who control legislation? Who control national police? Who control metro police? These controls receive a significant dedication in relation to political power and the citizens gets neglected in the process. This hampers delivery of peoples mandate, therefore hindering a core area of development. Whoever controls what, use whatever means to discredit the other in their favour to look good in the face of citizens and vice versa. This is chaotic means of governance. Energy and resources should solely be directed to citizens and improving the state of affairs.

This is a new democracy, a country needs radical means to change the status quo. All efforts need to be put in place to accomplish this course. There is no time to play pity grandstanding politics.

There is a huge, great, gigantic conflict in governance in the current three spheres of governance

An electoral reform is urgently required to merge elections into one and into one party state. A party elected must deliver in all spheres of government. Of course, in a given period of time as mandated by the people. If the party fails to achieve that, people are empowered to remove such party from government and put an alternative government that will be fit to deliver on their mandate. This course cannot be delayed, it needs immediate adoption to take its course. This is because the needs of the people cannot be delayed any further.

Party politics cannot take a centre stage anymore above people's needs. The nation cannot wait in vain to see majority of its people into active economy, getting employed, creating sustainable businesses, controlling their land, minerals and the means of production. Time is now or never. Polite approaches cannot be allowed anymore in adopted dispensations that do not serve the nation at large.

The people shall govern. It is time people must govern. One state party is what is required now. Lengthy debates, insults, casting aspersions, useless motions of no confidences should be removed.

In 2015 tertiary students took to the streets demanding free education. This turned into a national lengthy demonstration. While this outcry was in the streets and corridors of tertiary institutions. Political parties were busy throwing attacks at each other within state institutions, instead of putting together a resolve mechanism. Yes, a commission was established by government to look into the matter and the feasibility. No solution has jointly been put on the table by political parties and a decision have not been taken. What we are seeing is parties playing blaming and discrediting games in the process. This does nothing but disadvantage many of those who are on the outcry. Just an example of many other failing mechanisms on peoples needs under the current system.

The time has come for a One Party State. South Africa is Ready.

5

Structure of the economy

The structure of the economy is not properly aligned to the South African developmental requirements. The post apartheid state has absorbed an economy that was designed by the colonial system. The primary goal of this system was to extract wealth out of the country into colonial empires.

A coordinated system led by the captains of the system, did so brutally without any guilt of conscience. Putting white people as supreme and custodians of the system, while trading Black People as slaves to do hard labour and putting them at the very bottom of the system.

Blacks suppressed down the system to be owned by those who bought them to produce commodities for them. While this was inhuman and criminal against humanity, to trade a human being in exchange for money or anything. The system legalised this practise by passing laws to this effect. The system allowed brutality on Black People. This production machinery made only whites wealthy in the country.

In this way, an economy was created for trade between the legalised brigands, with no benefits to majority indigenous people of the land. The economic system grew to its peak levels over centuries cementing this crime. A humanity crime and economic crime giving birth to each other.

A crime that manifested into a global colonial system, creating very depth dependencies of how the world should function and attempting to create a global empire.

Control of this system was cemented in foreign lands of the coloniser. A control that still exist even today. Over the years since the dawn of democracy, so much little have changed to reflect required transformation to the economy structure. An amount of change to embody the country's developmental agenda. This does not mean the new state have done nothing to address transformation.

There is a bold trace of regulation and good intentions adopted to redress the economy.

An economy that needs balance to societal proportions. However, these interventions are developed on the principle of reconstruction and development. A principle pinned on the basis of reconciliation. A process that require both the perpetrator and the victim to commit to. So that justice can be achieved in a manner that will see both sides on an equal basis.

This includes inclusion of Black People in the main stream of the economy while whites relinquish unlawful accumulated wealth to bring about the required balance.

This is not happening because the white bourgeoisies do not want to relinquish its unlawful accumulation. This egotism is a danger to progressive development. Every piece of policy framework developed to address these imbalances is always counter acted by the white monopoly capital. To date, the Reconstruction and Development Policy (The RDP), The Growth, Employment and Redistribution Policy (GEAR), The Accelerated and Shared Growth Initiative South Africa (ASGISA) Policy, Mining Charters, The Land Redistribution Policy,

Every piece of policy
framework developed
to address these
imbalances is always
counter acted by the
white monopoly capital

The National Development Plan have not accomplished this mission. It is now over 20 years of democracy, The State and the nation are still battling to bring justice to this issue.

Blacks are still entrapped in the same position as it was during the colonial system. It is sad to imagine that the colonial system is still alive. Whites are still at the top of the economy. They still dominate the industries, they close black participation by enforcing collusions and cartels, price fixing and disallowing access to finance to Blacks. They created mergers and acquisitions systems and holding companies that are wide spread of goods and services.

Holding companies controlling closed commercial activities and representing only themselves. They created industry groups that require customised registrations to operate in a specific market. These groups operate on customised set of rules for participation into the markets.

These are all nothing but counter economic revolution as their criteria is designed to exclude majority of people. Systems enforced to counter the new democratic state policy on economic transformation. The system that continue to exclude Blacks from main commercial activities. Has the nation reconciled? What is the impact of policies that are reconciliatory based? Does the nation require a different economic redress model? Is it justifiable to continue to trade on a system created by the brigands? An answer to this is that economic freedom cannot be realised within a white created system and Blacks cannot be beggars of economic justice.

It is impossible because the country operates on a colonial economic model that is baseless to the urgent need of the African Agenda.

The existing economy reacts child like to any small piece of information that comes across, whether this information is fact or fiction, markets takes a particular direction. Media and social platforms disseminate information as it pleases and plays this card on the basis of freedom of speech. Not suggesting that all information is baseless, but let us take a swipe at some pointers. In August 2016, the media reports that the Minister of Finance is sanctioned to answer certain questions relating to a particular investigation.

Immediately the rand weakens and markets reacts negatively. This is just one piece of information and the consequences are dire and have an effect on the economy. Of course, the story has its own history.

Speculations are drawn and this affects many elements of the economy. This also elevates to a political space and different political characters play their political characters. The former MOF issues a statement that any charge of the incumbent Minister will collapse the economy. The cartel mayor of Johannesburg two days into office following his appointment issues a media statement against the president of the country.

The bottom line is how does all this affect ordinary citizens of the country. A technical analysis can be drawn into the implication of this matter. But can the new democracy afford this impact based on such pieces of information.

A new democracy that is still struggling to improve the lives of many underprivileged people cannot afford to focus its energy on uncontrollable elasticity of the economy.

An environment should be created to regulate and cap this kind of economic behaviour which cost millions of citizens millions and billions of rands as a result of this.

In a nutshell, this result in price increases of basic goods and services, loss of jobs amongst many basic life needs. This also highly affect Black Entrepreneurs who strive to make success of their businesses.

So more Black People get released from employment and Black Businesses collapse. An anti-progressive model that keeps Blacks on their knees in the same way as during the colonial era.

This is the economic system and structure that was created by the colonial state to milk wealth out of Africa. This still happens in a democratic state and does not respond to the basic requirements of an African Child. There is no way an African Child can strive under the current system.

Competition environment is very tightened and closed in its nature. white monopoly capital have made themselves giants of industries and in control of the countries minerals and land. They collude in their operations to set the trade agenda and the state have blunt teeth to deal with this.

Of course, there are institutions established to prosecute collusion crimes, however nothing has changed as these corporations are still conducting themselves in these undertakings. Regulation and prosecutions are not a problem for them because they pass the cost of fines imposed on them over to the end product price, if they ever get caught by authorities.

White monopoly capital control the trade system, cementing security of their position. This leaves majority of Blacks in the cold

Incorporation of this cost affect the end price that an ordinary citizen should pay for products and services. Therefore, paying more than necessary.

Who suffers at the end? It is ordinary citizens. Black business also suffers a great deal because it struggles to make in rows into the market. The country needs to change the way business is conducted domestically and globally.

White monopoly capital control the trade system, cementing security of their position. This leaves majority of Blacks in the cold. They control the banks and the entire financial sector. Access to finance is an absolute impossible mission to Blacks. There is no way a Black Child can infiltrate the markets. When it does, it is on the basis of a very small piece allocated for compliance to programmes such as Black Economic Empowerment (BEE).

But again, only the few benefit from BEE ventures and the gap between white control and black control remain hopeless to close. In fact, BEE cost an ordinary citizen more on goods and services because white corporations pass over the BEE cost back to prices of goods and services. So an ordinary person on the ground unintentionally suffers a great deal as a result of this initiative.

Little have been done to curtail this practice. Yes, again, there are institutions established to monitor this unscrupulous behaviour to protect consumers against this abuse. However existing strategies seems to be reactive and behind in their nature towards the white monopoly capital. This makes existing strategies ineffective to put a stop to this practice.

A Radical African Economic Reform is required to deal with the nature of business in our boundaries. New African rules of engagements are required. New terms and conditions are required. African models are required and bi-lateral trades should be dominated by the African model.

Why should the nation be subjected to value its minerals such as gold in foreign lands currency? Minerals should be valued and traded in own currency. The country does not have control over other states currencies. The country can only control its own currency despite dependencies on exchange rates.

But again, it should be remembered who owns these corporations that exploit the nations' minerals. Of course, they are not South African companies.

White supremacy
continues to steal from
the Black nation, right in
front of her liberated eyes

This model is not
sustainable. It is bound to
cause a national unrest
and more divisions
between the nation. It is
absolutely not
contributing to nation
building

Minerals are exploited by foreign nationals at foreign currencies in our own land. More than 20 years of democracy, this is still a game in hand. This was a very sore pain during the colonial period, but it is even more of a pain when still happening in a post-apartheid state.

What must it take for an african child to benefit from ownership of its own minerals? White supremacy continues to steal from the Black nation, right in front of her liberated eyes.

Billions of rands are taken out of the country unaccounted for. Billions of rands which should be benefiting millions of Black people. It is a crime to commit theft in a country, in contrary no prosecutions are conducted against the owners of these companies. They continue to enjoy big profits out of these corrupt acts.

This model is not sustainable. It is bound to cause a national unrest and more divisions between the nation. It is absolutely not contributing to nation building.

It is ok if the 1994 dispensation was negotiated in a manner that is was, but if the dispensation is not serving the majority people of the country, it should be terminated and altered. New rules of engagements are required. We still see an increasing activity by organised labour.

This means very little if not anything has changed in the labour market.

We should be seeing more advanced organised labour as a symbol of reformed economy. Labour continue to receive very little compensation while prices of goods and services soars. Conditions of employment are still reported as below standard. On the opposite side the white monopoly capital put blame on labour laws. That it finds it difficult to conduct business, yet they still make big profits.

The level of misreporting is increasing to hide actual company performance levels. These are reports of incorrect invoicing by corporations to hide their correct state of affairs. A sad and sore conduct in a new democracy. Majority of people suffer out of this conduct. The unemployed remain unemployed, the employed get retrenched, yet everyone have to pay high prices of goods and services emanating out of this conduct and Black business stay out of business.

Introduction of drastic trade and economic reforms is crucial. Enforcement of spaces where Blacks can equally compete and nationalisation of strategic sectors needs yesterday implementation. Radical redistribution of land to boost economic activity must be embarked on.

The state is characterised by spaces where Blacks remain marginalised even if they have an excellent innovation. The first problem is funding to finance their initiative. Banks do not lend to Black people with no commercial records. Even if they have a sound investment initiative. Other funding institutions do not have sufficient funds to support black business. Therefore, entry into markets is very limited and an impossible mission.

All sectors of the economy are untransformed. For example, construction is a high capital intensive operation. However, there are Blacks who can embark on this mission on their own. But the system requires construction of a fence wall before qualifying to construct a house.

By the time Blacks get to construct big projects, whites will be constructing mega-mega projects. Blacks will always play a catch up to whites. It does not make sense. The country have qualified Black engineers, architects, quantity surveyors, project managers. The system forces them to practice in engineering firms before they are fully admitted. These are white owned firms.

All sectors of the economy
are untransformed

Why not pull these resources in a development approach and start making things happen? But again, the system is such that from a human development side, its better of an option to remain with a captured system than to operate outside it.

By the time a person earns an income, is financial dependent. A system that sustain white supremacy. Mining sector, manufacturing, and other sectors are in the same pattern. Management and design meetings are still dominated by whites. In most cases whites only. While Black people are found on the ground. When government announces budgets, especially on infrastructure, one can only imagine where state money is going. To white corporations. So, when government announces a R500 billion infrastructure budget, government is actually saying white corporations you are now going to be R500 billion richer. Time has come where the nation should be saying the budget is R500 billion and R450 billions of it is going to Black business. This is real development of the nation. A struggle fought over many decades for the liberation of the nation. Gross Domestic Product (GDP) in the country is growing at about 2.9% and the country is ranked 30th in the GDP ranking. The country has a population of 55 million people, of which over 80% is black population. 79% of land is privately owned by white people. Only 8% of the population is white. The GDP in real value is 4.5 trillion rands. Almost all in the hands of white people.

Government is putting up a stimulating environment to grow the GDP to a double value. If inequalities and imbalances are not addressed fearlessly, unashamedly and radically, in the next 10 to 15 years, whites will own double the GDP to the value of over 10 trillion rands. This is a recipe for disaster, a time bomb and a nation waiting to explode.

With quarter of the economic population being unemployed, Blacks in particular, it cannot be right that the nation can say that there is nothing wrong here. We are talking over 20 years of democracy. Millions of Black people are still trapped in poverty, suffering and oppressed under this economic structure that is not african. 8% of the population own 79% of land and the GDP in trillions of rands. 80% of blacks own only 13% of land while the state only own 14%. Haaikhona this cannot be right.

Food production and security of majority of people is in the hands of the 8%. This is a disaster.

It cannot be right that the breath of the 80% population is in the hands of the 8%. The struggle in the country was aimed at reversing this crime and injustice. The country is still faced with the same colonial system. Nothing is coming out of the 8% to reform the status quo.

Policies have been developed in line with the constitution but the reality is that the 8% does not want to play part in these initiatives. While the country has these problems, government is always lured to invite more foreign investments to cement this practice. This is done in the name of growth and development, but it actually triples white supremacy. This is not a suggestion that foreign investments are not good initiatives. But the balance between ownership, control, and driving the economy is benefiting the 8% more than the 80% and the 25% unemployed.

There is so much wealth in the country, enough to address the imbalances, but this wealth is in the hands of the 8%. There is no machinery to redress this.

The framework available is a reconciliatory framework that is one sided. People have power and people can use their power to redress these issues. The power of the people is not only in the ballot box, as we are always made to believe.

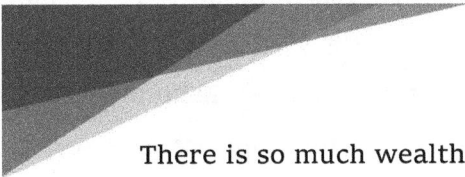

There is so much wealth in the country,
enough to address the imbalances, but
this wealth is in the hands of the 8%

People cannot wait for other centuries for these issues to be corrected. The time is now. The 80% cannot be let to feel guilt of the conceptualised pain of the 8%. What about the pain of the 80%. Which one is greater and deadly? At least the pain of the 8% is a shared pain unlike the pain of the 80% which is not altogether a shared pain. The pain of thousands of tertiary students on high institutions fees is an isolated pain. An institutionalised mechanism to exclude Blacks from tertiary education. Leaving them at the bottom of nowhere. We have since now, not seen the 8% pledging support for the course of no fees programmes. The pain of people living in squatter camps is an isolated pain, we have not seen the 8% pledging support to this pain.

The pain of the low income earners is an isolated pain, we do not see the 8% pledging support to this pain. They always have to be forced to pay decent wages, and they refuse. In circumstances where they concede, they retrench Blacks months after conceding. This is the pain left to the 80% to live with alone. It cannot be right to continue like this. Pain kills, and the truth is that it has killed many in many forms.

Yes, it is true that there are Blacks whose lives have improved. They have migrated into a new defined class called the middle class. Yes, it is true, there are Black people who started and are running successful businesses. Yes, there are philanthropy programmes that give back to the needy and corporate social initiatives that contribute to the needy. Yes, there are government policies that enable this environment to exist and contribute to the needy.

But the majority are still trapped in poor situations. The social and welfare structure is not out of the red zone. The country's welfare budget increase in billions year after year and there is a suggestion that the country has become a welfare state.

While this problem is growing, the economy is reported to be shrinking. Do we have the right kind of an economic structure? The current one does not respond to the plight of the people. Let us look at the pointers. All political parties are still campaigning on the improvement of the lives of the people. So, the problem still exists.

There has now been talks about the nation having to engage in the ECONOMIC CODESA. The discussion on this is in the open and various parties, individuals and formations are at dialogue on this phenomenon. We are seeing political leaders and analysts arguing about an economic CODESA. The reality is, the initial CODESA should have addressed these issues. Secondly the problem is not whether we need an economic CODESA or not, the 8% simply does not want to transform the economy. They do not want to comply with set transformation targets and legislative requirements. The 80% cannot go back to the 8% to negotiate their right of decent living. That option was exercised during the initial CODESA. The 80% just have to take what is rightfully theirs as human beings.

It is their right to live a decent life. The constitution also pins on this right. Economic structural reforms in this manner cannot be negotiated any longer. Not having suffered over 340 years of oppression. This right had been negotiated, even when there was no need to negotiate it. It just has to be claimed. Land redistribution is not an option, wealth redistribution is not an option, decent wages and working conditions is not an option, development of Black entrepreneurship is not an option, decent housing and human settlements is not an option, decent water and sanitation is not an option, decent and affordable electricity is not an option, rural development is not an option, free education is not an option. The time is now now now not tomorrow.

6

Economic Evolution

The structure of the economy characterises the state affairs of South African economy. It highlights an economic system that has less impact on the ordinary citizen. Including the required reforms necessary to radically change the status quo, in order to radically improve the lives of millions of South Africans. While it is imperative to have an economic shift that fit an african agenda, it is also fair to look at the evolution of the South African economy post the apartheid era. Many economists and policy makers disagree on the types of policies needed to attain different economic goals, however the following are the basic economic goals that are accepted in different societies:

Economic freedom

Economic growth

Full employment

Price level stability

Equitable income distribution

Balance of trade and payments

Economic efficiency and security

An era of democracy in saw some of the apartheid policies being abolished. The new state introduced new policies that aimed at achieving socio-economic objectives. Development of the nation being at its core. This shift had an impact on the performance of the economy. Noting that amongst other things the economy is intended to raise sustainable living standards of the population and reduce poverty. Therefore, the country developed various economic policies aimed at economic development and its objectives were to create jobs, eliminate poverty, reduce inequalities and grow the wealth of the country and its majority people.

In 1995 the new government estimated that approximately 28% of households and 48% of the population were living below the poverty line. Recent reports indicate that poverty remain a huge problem, though improvements are being noted.

The key to achievement of economic development was to create a macro-economic stability, steady trade reform, improved trade access, increased competitiveness, encourage foreign direct investment and small medium macro enterprises.

Various socio-economic policies were developed to drive economic stability, change and growth.

Amongst them being Reconstruction and Development Programme (RDP, developed in 1994), Growth Employment and Redistribution (GEAR, aimed at maintaining annual economic growth at 6%), Accelerated and Shared Growth Initiative South Africa (ASGISA, aimed at halving poverty and unemployment by 2014, averaging

However, this economic boost largely benefited white monopoly capital and foreign investors and continue to do so. On the other side the unemployment levels still remained high, reflecting largely the Black population annual GDP growth of above 4% between 2005 and 2009, and 6% between 2010 and 2014) and New Growth Path (NGP, aimed at creating employment, reducing unemployment from 25% to 15% by 2020 and reducing the inequality gap).

To support these economic policies, the Reserve Bank developed and adopted a monetary policy of inflation targeting aimed at containing the inflation between 3 and 6 percent. South African economy post 1994 evolved from an era among other things with no foreign exchange reserves, very high public debt, high inflation levels, very few in the population actively participating in the economy (largely whites), high unemployment levels etc.

During the period 1994 and 2001, the country was successful in stabilising the economy, boosting domestic and foreign investment which was critical in driving economic growth.

The period 2000 and beyond enjoyed an increase in the economic activity within the country. Investment rose, inflation and interest rates declined rapidly.

However, this economic boost largely benefited white monopoly capital and foreign investors and continue to do so. On the other side the unemployment levels still remained high, reflecting largely the Black population.

South African economy is ranked by international economic institutions such as the World Bank and the International Monetary Fund as the upper middle income economy, and referred to as the developing economy.

Gross Domestic Product indicates a steady growth since 1994 with an average growth above 2%. This trend though saw a decline in 2009 due to global economic crises and drew the economy into recession.

Though many economic characters classified the economic activity early as the economy being in recession. Government argued that the country was not in recession yet and explained the technical performance and indicators which informs the economy being in recession. It argued that the country will technically be in recession if it realised two consecutive periods of negative growth.

This realisation was seen later in a year during May 2009. This occurrence resulted in about a million jobs being lost due to decline in demand of goods and services, mostly in the construction, retail and services sectors.

The country's monetary policy staged a vital role in rescuing the economy out of recession.

The fiscal easing was seen as the largest among the G20 countries. As a result, was able to mobilise resources in support of the economy without compromising future growth and service delivery.

The remaining challenge was to streamline the financial and monetary policies to reduce the fiscal deficit in order to allow for resources to be channelled through development agenda than to service debt over a prolonged period. The period 2000 to 2016 is characterised by productivity improvement in certain sectors, but at the same time a decline in output in certain industries.

The labour cost is recorded as being high in comparison to other developing economies. White monopoly capital always insists on low earnings in defiance to better and deserving wages for the majority. Unemployment remains a challenge for the country, having reached a top level of 31% in 2003. Dropping to about 23% in 2007 and currently standing at 26%. This trend indicates that the economy has not grown to its required capacity to be able to absorb majority of the population and improve the economic activity.

While it can be argued that, its strength was able to quickly pull it out of recession and steadily grew. It continues to benefit the minority of the population dominated by whites and the colonial economies. While the majority Black population, about 23 million are still

These trends raised a notion in 2003 that the country has two parallel economies within one country trapped under the poverty line. These trends raised a notion in 2003 that the country has two parallel economies within one country. The first economy and the second economy.

The first economy characterised by:

its integration to the global market;

its capacity to export manufactured goods and primary commodities; and

its incorporation of only the minority of the population.

The second economy characterised by:

under-development;

contributes little to GDP;

has weak social capital;

incorporates the poorest population who do not directly benefit from the advanced sectors of South African economy;

is structurally disconnected from the first and global economies; and is incapable of self-generated growth.

Macro-economic problems still faced by the country are high unemployment rate, high income inequalities, high poverty levels, poor economic growth, high prices of goods and services etc. These are nations deep routed wounds unable to heal regardless of economic policies that were developed and implemented over the period.

The World Economic Forum 2016 report on Global Competitiveness indicates that the county's economic competitiveness has been deteriorating since 2009/10 where it ranked 45 out of 140 economies. The following years until 2014/15 it dropped to reach a ranking of 56, signalling a weakening position in relation to competitiveness with other economies. However, its performance showed an improvement in 2016 with a ranking of 49. The economy still maintains a top half ranking and remains the highest ranked economy in Sub-Saharan Africa.

The most perceived weaknesses holding back the competitiveness of the economy are:

Restrictive labour regulation

Inefficient government bureaucracy

Inadequate supply of infrastructure

Policy stability

Inadequate educated workforce

Crime and theft

Corruption

Poor work ethic in labour force

Access to finance

Insufficient capacity to innovate

Tax rates

Foreign currency regulation

Complexity of tax regulations

Inflation

Poor public health

Perceived factors that upheld the position of the economy are:

Increased activity on ICT- especially higher internet bandwidth

Improvement on innovation, establishing the economy as the region's most innovative

Hosting of the continent's most efficient financial markets

Benefits from sound goods market

Efficient transport infrastructure

Strong institutions, particularly property rights

Robust and independent legal framework

The economy grew over the period years 2000 to 2016. However, the growth is very slow and adversely below a set growth target. It also fails to achieve its developmental goals of raising sustainable living standards of majority of the population, eliminating poverty, creating jobs, closing inequality gaps, and growing the wealth of the country. These remain a problem and the biggest challenge. Not only of government but of society to resolve. Leaving the first economy to exist in parallel to the second economy.

The recession during 2009 further decelerated the economic growth. Corruption, rising prices of goods and services and other related factors also contributes to slower growth. The economy continues to benefit the minority of the population. Largely white population and colonial economies, and leaving majority of the population marginalised. The unemployment levels remain intolerably high and the poverty situation in the country does not improve.

The economic and labour policies remain disintegrated. But largely white monopoly capital remains defiant to the societal developmental agenda.

The economic system needs to be radically changed without fear. The first and second economies need to integrate. Racism in the first economy need to be dealt with and completely collapsed. Any means of anti-Black and Black exclusions that includes cartels, collusions and price fixing need to be banished unashamedly so. Not in the form of fines that eventually find themselves into end prices of goods and services. Corruption needs to be dealt with decisively at all levels.

7

The Brigands

The attempt by the brigands to own the world. They ventured into a mission to steal minerals from foreign lands and extract its worth into their lands to create wealth and control the world. Attempting to subject all nations in the universe under their control.

They forced themselves into lands with oil, gas, gold, diamond and many other minerals.

In the endeavour to obtain the desired control, the brigands turned against each other. This created wars and millions of ordinary civilians innocently and defencelessly die as a result. They created systems of trade for such minerals, that installed control in their remote lands. They decide how much and when to extract and what price to sell these minerals. Oil not an isolated controlled commodity is one example of how the brigands invaded the oil lands and created oil fields. Wars ensued in pursue of this task. Military machinery became core to winning the battle of control. This machinery is still in motion to preserve desired controls. Not only military oversee this control but also institutions and systems are installed to facilitate movement of these commodities and monies related to it. An institutionalised method of foreign control over the world.

Some of these institutions are trade exchanges launched in strategic locations. None of these are found in any parts of Africa. They are governed by brigands of industries and do not include representation from producing nations. None of the governors are from the nations where these minerals are extracted from. Foreign corporations were installed in mineral depository lands to extract these minerals. Using owning lands civilians as slavery labour. The brigands gather together and decide on the rise and drop of prices of these minerals depending on

Even after independence
in these states that were
colonized, it is still
impossible to benefit
wealth out of the nations
minerals. This is because
independence states
continue to allow their
minerals to be traded in
ancient created forms of
trade. A trade created by
the brigands to suit their
mission

the strategies suiting their appetite. A process completely closed to the few of them yet affecting multi-billions of the world citizens. They trade these minerals in a form of future contracts. A process of buying a commodity at today's price for delivery in months to come. Thereafter selling back the commodities at exorbitant prices. A price determined only in one state currency.

Over the years we have witnessed oil prices ranging between $50 and $150 per barrel. Wealth creation out of these commodities is centralised to these power houses. A form of cartel that stands against all forms of good competition principles. Mineral owning nations are unable to absorb wealth out of their own minerals simply because they do not have control over them.

Even after independence in these states that were colonized, it is still impossible to benefit wealth out of the nations minerals. This is because independence states continue to allow their minerals to be traded in ancient created forms of trade. A trade created by the brigands to suit their mission. This system was not created to benefit the rightful custodians of minerals. It will never decolonize independence states from economic bondages. Under these systems millions of rightful custodians are bound to be trapped in slavery, cheap labour, unemployment, poverty, inequality and oppression for many centuries to come. Unless these are dismantled in any form it takes, the situation in custodian lands is bound to stay the same and deteriorate over time.

The universal labour statistics attest to this. The mining companies exploring these minerals are still the colonial institutions created by the colonial system. They are refusing to transform and are stubbornly still using their same colonial means of production.

Cheap labour is an order of the day and they misrepresent their production outputs and profits to avoid paying taxes. Taxes that should be benefiting the nations in their developmental programmes. Price transfers and illicit financial flows has become an order of the day. A process they use to illegally move monies out of countries unaccounted.

More than 50 billion US dollars is reported to be leaving the African Continent year on year unaccounted. A region rich of minerals yet still trapped in unbearable poverty, unemployment, inequality and sickness. Trillions of rands leave the custodian lands unaccounted instead of eradicating poverty, unemployment, inequality and sickness. This affect substantially the performance of

Trillions of rands leave the
custodian lands unaccounted
instead of eradicating poverty,
unemployment, inequality and
sickness

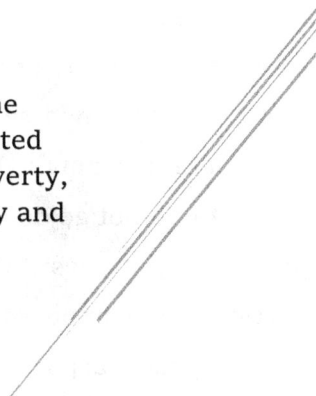

custodian nations, leaving them as under developing economies. Economies that continue to require financial boosting from the brigands. These boosting comes with conditions which put strain on custodian nations and resulting in high dependency on foreign lands. Brigands keeping the superior lords status over custodian nations.

These boosts come in forms of foreign loans to fund infrastructure developments. A process of ensuring that foreign companies dominate the markets and dictate terms and conditions of trade. They leave nations without available budget to fund its own development. A chunk of the budget gets diverted to honouring foreign debt. Subjecting the nation to continue to bow before the foreign land as their lord.

For the brigands, it is about winning at all cost. You cannot beat them in their home ground. Their home ground is made out of their own rules. You cannot beat them with their own rules. You have to change the game plan and create new rules if you want to beat them. But hey, that will not go down easily with them. That is where the military comes in and victimisation of civilians. Sanctions gets imposed on nations seen as disobedient with a crystal purpose to starve them. It is unbelievable that sanctions can only be imposed by the colonial states.

The same states that will plead foreign aid in devastated nations are the same states that will put the nation in devastation.

Africa should be for Africans. Africans know best how to live and sustain their livelihood. But to some extent a doctrine to believe they cannot live without the colonial states creeps in. There is nothing wrong with fair collaboration, but there is everything wrong with colonial domination. There is everything wrong with white domination and white monopoly capital.

Whites always misconstrue black patience and humanity as weak. The apartheid state and many forms of imperialism did so for many years and still in their mind think black is weak. If they could be put down with all their machinery. Nothing will stop Africa to prosper. Nothing will stop the south to prosper and acquire ownership of its wealth.

When that time comes, there will not be an opportunity for economy integration because of refusal to reconcile till to this day. The nation will reconstruct purely on its own rules. The nation will own and control its land, minerals and the means of production. The nation shall not remain in poor conditions forever. The nation does not need foreign rules to reconstruct its survival. The nation does not need brigands trade exchanges and chambers to redirect its course. They shall be abolished. New rules will be drawn. The only shortcome is to believe that the society can only live out of brigands created rules. Africa Rise. Africa Rise.

Why must Africa be controlled by institutions dominated by greed and corruption. These institutions are well known for power battles within its ranks and fights over mineral supply.

These spread over by opening different other trading exchanges and migrating them between strategic cities. Coming with all sort of fierce, manipulation, bribes and corruption. But one thing for sure, it was done so to keep dominance and control. A centralised form of control and closing down on any threat competition.

Of course, regulation and time difference became a major issue in keeping up with this control. Strategic deployments had to be made in these remote exchanges and trading times fixed. For example, gold exchange daily fixed times are 10:30am and 14:30pm. When other colonisers open for trade, other colonisers are sleeping. When sleeping colonisers motion into its trading hours, the awake colonisers gets to bed. So, a harmonised system

Why must Africa be controlled by institutions dominated by greed and corruption. These institutions are well known for power battles within its ranks and fights over mineral supply is created in fixing times to benefit the big boys. Rules they created themselves. These are also the times their currency is at its peak, so it would give them a much reality value of their trades. Everybody else just have to follow suit. Everybody including the owners of minerals.

South Africa is no exception to this. With its gold, diamonds, platinum, silver....It is subjected to this system. Well those that control the means of production locally are extensions of the lords from their lands. Their mandate locally is to extract as much as possible locally. Influence regulation to suit their course. Manipulate local currency to export at desired rates and re-manipulate currency to import at desired rates. Government regulation favours them to the extreme, where it does not, they defy it and no one is held to account.

South African economy is largely based on these brigades' rules. Rules created to benefit the rulers and not the majority citizens. This is the reason transformation is not happening in these sectors. Despite a multiple of mining charters developed by government. South Africa has not transformed in these sectors and transformation will not see the daylight under the brigades' rules.

Rules that include the phenomenon of a state capture. A phenomenon hitting a tipping point in the corridors of the state. Co-option of powerful individuals within the circles of the state. It is no secret that these individuals have been offered free and vendor shareholdings in the brigands corporations. They have been co-opted as non-executive directors and chairpersons of these power houses. So, the voice and the political will to dismantle these rules have been diluted. Foreign control is being affirmed. While this affirmation enjoys its stay, millions of citizens continue to suffer under this regime. Hopes for the upliftment of the lives of Black people gets reduced day after day, and a fight over better wages and living conditions become an increasing and deadly activity.

The beneficiation programme is nothing but just a hymn book only for government to its people. This hymn book is not included in the brigands orchestra, and they are not about to include it. Instead of implementing the beneficiation programme they report a decline in productivity.

For many years before democracy, South Africa was ranked number 1 country in the production of gold. Leading all nations. Post democracy, production output is reported as declining and the country is now ranked 11 amongst gold producing countries.

What is the chance of Blacks accessing finance from the financial sector for projects that are reported as not financially viable?

Labour cost and the overall cost of mining is reported high. The mining processes and machinery is also reported as long having reached its lifespan. Mineral exploration is also reported as having reached its depletion levels.

Has brigandy extracted all the countries minerals? Is this a notion created to divert attention to the nation not to bother to pursue exploration? "There's nothing left for you to explore", do not bother. Then this means the nation has to remain poor. What is the chance of Blacks accessing finance from the financial sector for projects that are reported as not financially viable? A sector also controlled by them, with rules written by them and land owned by them. A system of closed control and no one must come into their territory. If then things are that doomy, why do we see an increase in price transfers, misinvoicing, illicit financial flows. Why billions of rands leave the country unaccounted for. Where do these billions come from? Why mergers and acquisitions happening amongst themselves? Why are they still holding on to goldfields?

Their share prices reached its lowest in 2015 as labour embarked on a strike for better wages and living conditions. Projecting a dying sector and emphasizing that they cannot afford requested wage increases and that they were not sustainable. A settlement was reached prior to December. Astonishingly share prices recovered immediately after the US Federal Reserve Bank hiked interest rates on 16 December 2015. Thereafter share prices reaching their highest, three months later in 2016. Boosted further by the UK referendum on Brexit.

This is a symbol of a healthy sector within a white monopoly capital. But purposefully reported as a dying sector in the eyes of Blacks, to continue to exclude Blacks from pursuing access to this sector. The platinum sector, the steel sector, the petroleum sector trailed on the same pattern. These are not new trading tactics. Some of these were reported in 2007 with oil being hidden in ocean and offshore storages to control the price of oil and petroleum at a later stage. Hiding tactics were applied to cover up the volumes of oil available. Applying the demand and supply rules would determine the price within which to pay for oil. This happened under the umbrella of collaborations and cartels and its primary purpose was monopoly control and huge profit takings. This affects the world in general and South Africa is no exception. The end user at the filling station gets affected by this tactic and it affects performance of the nations economy.

A fearless team of leaders is required to fearlessly and shamelessly take on this challenge. A patriotic nation is required to ensure that this happens. This is possible because the power is bestowed upon the nation to drive that change

If the country does not get hold of its minerals, it remains a puppet to global economic theatre show.

Ownership of the countries land, minerals, means of production and wealth will give the country a required boost to position itself better on a global stage. This will benefit millions and millions of people of this country. It will turn the sluggish economic situation into a prospering nation economy.

But this cannot happen under the old rules. New rules of engagement are required. Radical economic reforms are required. Regulations that are enforceable are required. A fearless team of leaders is required to fearlessly and shamelessly take on this challenge. A patriotic nation is required to ensure that this happens. This is possible because the power is bestowed upon the nation to drive that change.

No more should the nation live under economic criminal rules. All shacks shall be abolished and decent housing with proper water, sanitation and electricity shall be owned by each and every citizen. Education shall be free. Equal access to economic sectors shall be achieved. Land and its minerals shall return to its people. Black business shall prosper. Citizens shall be paid best wages. Innovation shall be an order of the day on our soil.

Health care shall be of high quality to all. Consumers shall pay correct prices for goods and services and not manipulated prices. Peace and Stability shall reign on our shores. Blacks will assume their rightful places on planet. No one will go to bed without food. Africa shall Rise. Africa is on the Rise.

8

Changing Gears

It is so remarkable that today the nation is tackling the issue of the economy. The nation is raising its voice on the issue and taking a particular course. It is so remarkable that thousands of vibrant young Black people, is a generation that is saying "we want to find space in this economic space". These voices are true and genuine to the course. These voices cannot be suppressed in any form or another. The nation is vibrantly yearning for economic freedom. From a Black child to a Black child, from an

African to an African. It is a Black Child's time. It is an African Child time. This is the time to charter a way forward. A way forward of making sure that the economically excluded majority become authors of their future.

Fathers and Mothers of the nation, under very difficult times made sure that children had something to eat at night. They made sure that they provide the little they had, to make sure that a soul never goes to bed without food.

It is not food that our children will be eating when the economic encounter succeed, and for many years to come. It was not food that anyone would go out and brag that they had chicken or meat. It was either hard porridge and water.

But what is very important is that, that upbringing has shaped the generation under it. An upbringing under apartheid and bantu education has shaped the generation to demonstrate that they are true liberators of themselves. That they have so much power to liberate themselves and that they are better. No one and nobody can define how good they are. Who would have thought that today a Black child would be talking about the issue of national economy

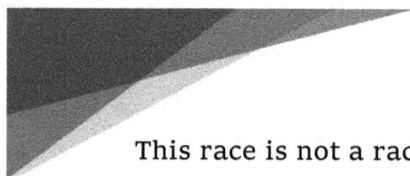

This race is not a race that can be completed in seconds. It is not a 100m race

The yearning generation believe and know that what they are doing is right. Still under these very difficult times, the today generation is taking its position to occupy the economic space. They endeavour to run successful businesses.

There is indeed a traceable progress delivered by democracy, however so much needs to be done to address the disparities. As this work take its course, it should be thoughtful that business calls for discipline. You cannot want to be in business if you are not responsible, not committed and not disciplined. You only have a dream. A dream is not good enough if you are not fighting for your dream to come true. If you are in business, avoid becoming a general businessperson. Dream big but know the journey of finally getting to the final line. This race is not a race that can be completed in seconds. It is not a 100m race.

It is very important to identify a niche and avoid what happens in general. Avoid investing energy in businesses that are not synergetic to each other. This usually happens because of a rage race of accumulating wealth without a base. That is one thing that need to be avoided at all cost. Never chase deals without direction. Remain as a leader and own strategy. Never focus on low hanging fruits because they are within reach of everyone. Take bold steps to be in a position to compete against the multi-nationals. Make yourself indispensable, make yourself indispensable to the person you see when you look yourself in the mirror. And tell that person, you have not seen nothing yet. But all of that is only achievable if you are responsible, diligent, remain focused, and follow your dream.

The other point that is fundamental in business is that all its traits is based on personalities. You become a brand. The hallmark of your business must be around you. That when people see you, they see your business. Then you know, you are known like them who made their name during the colonial period. We still refer to them as owners of certain corporations. We talk about them as if they own 100% of those corporations, even though they have sold all their stake in those corporations. So how you behave in darkness, in light, reflects on you. You need to guard jealousy of who you are.

Entrepreneurs must know and accept that they are never job seekers, they are job creators.

It is so unfortunate in our country that the Small Medium Micro Enterprises (SMME's) have not taken its rightful position in the economy.

It is so unfortunate in our country that the Small Medium Micro Enterprises (SMME's) have not taken its rightful position in the economy if you look at the economies of the world, economies of Japan, economies of China, economies of Britain, economies of Germany, including America whose had an economic slump. Who is pulling America out of an economic slump? It is the SMME's. These enterprises are the engine of any economy. They should be given a priority because they are the ones who create more jobs. It is not big companies.

Big companies are there to make sure that the economy still moves. But they are also the ones that squeeze small business. It is still good to be an SMME because you can still move faster, if you are an elephant, you move slow. Imagine pushing an elephant up the staircase, it will crush. Today if you look all over the world, the fastest growing economies, the top 10. Seven of them are in Africa. That is why SMME's should focus in investing in this space. Africa has had relations with the colonial powers, but the colonial powers have not helped Africa. Instead the nations have been left behind. Infrastructure is almost non-existence. That is an opportunity to be pursued. It is not that opportunities are only available in mining.

People are still buying groceries from Europe. Even fruits and vegetables gets flown into the continent.

South Africa have vast track of land, and even in the continent. Food security is very critical to our livelihood and it is self-supporting, and sustainability is key. South Africa were the bread basket of its own economy. It even used to export maize. Today maize is imported. This is a great opportunity. The nation need to get involved aggressively in agriculture.

Rice is also a basic need and the continent is relying heavily on the Asian side for supply. But they have their challenges relating to land, production and supply. In most instances when they face these challenges, they resort to Africa for sourcing solutions. The continent has its own capacity in rice production, and this is another opportunity for exploration.

The same thing in Sudan. They export about 6million herd of cattle. These are some of the opportunities that offer great benefit. There are vast opportunities that are available in the continent. Health care is one existing opportunity. Our problem is that we do not want to become traders, yet commodities are the ones that have made people wealthy. There is a richest man in the continent. His business was distribution of flower and maize.

He used the money that he made in the flower and maize industry to build himself a massive business in cement. Today he is the biggest manufacturer of cement. If we were to ask him today, what is his primary business, yet he is involved in financial services, food security, he will tell you I'm Mr Cement. Why has he chosen cement? Because he saw that Africa has lacked behind in infrastructure and there will be more money spent in infrastructure, roads to be built, hospitals, houses to be built for a long long time. He has identified a niche.

About a decade ago there were talks about power shortage that was going to be experienced in the future. Then one could identify a niche and say there will be opportunities in power generation. This is not a problem faced only by South Africa. Look at the map from the world bank that shows Europe at night. What you notice from the map is that when you fly over Europe at night, it is like day time. But when you fly over Africa at night, its dark. Why do they call Africa a dark continent? Is it because of the pigment of peoples' skin? It is because of the shortage of power. God has blessed Africa with rare and valuable minerals. Both solid and liquid, oil and mining. But you cannot extract them if you do not have power. The economy without electricity cannot triple.

Those who spotted an opportunity then, today are participating in the power generating initiatives. They would be supplying electricity.

The super powers have been involved in many feuds particularly around west Africa, as well as in the middle east. Because of the shortage of oil in their region to power their economy. They realised that they have to make alliances in the oil fields because they wanted their oil, in spite of violation of human rights and abuses. They had to condone it and turn a blind eye on those violations because of their economy survival. Like they turned a blind eye on apartheid when it suited them in their fight against communism.

In 2006 they committed to creating a great economy. What is a great economy? An economy fit to make sure that they deal with the issue around energy security. In so doing they invested tons of money to explore innovative opportunities. Today they are self-sufficient with energy that is even able to power motor cars. Gone are the days that they have to become friends with people because they want oil. South Africa have shale gas. It should explore opportunities within and not give it to foreign lands.

The society deserves the
opportunity. A new participation
programme is required

Government should give it to the nation, who should then strategically form partnerships. When
you talk about the security of the economy of the country, the vanguards are the residents and the citizens of that country. Solutions must be given to them so that they can be able to deal with the risk that is at hand.

Today the colonial cords in democracy are going all out about how this resource is not going to work in the country and present a dangerous side of it. That is because they want to control the future and implementation of this opportunity. If the nation is going to be silent and not join in the fight on shale gas. Majority will have no say in how much it will cost to fill up their cars in the future. The society deserves the opportunity. A new participation programme is required.

Not like the one where a white corporation is specialising in food packaging. Ninety percent of the food they package is food consumed by Blacks, packaged by whites. There is no white that consume these products. This is a food security issue.

Foreign giants moved in to buy the business and the company is now owned in foreign land. If you have food production without Black involvement, it is like having oil without local involvement. And that is a problem that needs to be resolved by the country and the continent.

9

Transmuting Power

One cannot begin to imagine the kind of livelihood the humankind ought to have. What are the holding pillars enabling the kind of life that is sufficient for our development? Our body and soul need natural cultivation as our daily intake. The creation provides all that we need to survive without pain and suffering.

The land, its minerals, the forest, the waters, the mountains, the air we breathe, the skies and the natural relationship of all these, forms the body of this creation. A creation for humankind and its survival. The beauty and richness of it is so unimaginable.

A creation for humankind. How did the humankind find itself in conflict of this creation? Did it lose relation with itself? How did humankind rob the creation of its purpose to feed humanity? How did it assume powerful ownership of this creation? People in the land are in so much conflict over personal ownership, that dozens of its own suffer the consequences. This ownership is busy destroying the creation and reducing life to an obstacle over control.

Peace and harmony have been substituted with hatred and exploitation. The man-made power taking over the universe. The power that destroys and enriching only the self-proclaimed warriors. The power that has captured and corrupted mankind. Looking at the world from an imaginable distance, a livelihood distance of our lives. We see humanity with a different eye. We see the richness of the creation and its abundance to cater for all humankind. The delicacy of a soul.

Another eye sees greed, brutality, suffering, pain and death. The creed of human possession and dispossession by any form of power that destroys. This is the ideology of power. The man-made power. The power that made billions of civilians trapped in poverty, sickness, slavery and many forms of oppression.

Peace and harmony have
been substituted with
hatred and exploitation.
The man-made power
taking over the
universe. The power
that destroys and
enriching only the self-
proclaimed warriors

The power that gives joy to those who rides on this power. The power to rule nations.

However, this is not alpha and omega power. There is power to liberate, the power to free the economic trappings, the power to equal living between citizens, nations and races, the power to equal economic opportunities, the power to equal access to nations wealth, the power to equal health and education standards, but most importantly the power within humanity to our own liberation. The power imbedded in our weakness. A weakness of oppression, suppression, exclusion from many forms of human upliftment. A weakness inscribed by the imperial and colonial system, which still occupy many forms of life. The kind of power in weakness that was used to overthrow the mighty colonial governments. Although not enough to overthrow the colonial powers. This power is enough to demolish the last colonial fibre in our system.

We cannot help to notice the many killings that are happening around the world, the consumption of revenge, resentment, wounding instead of gratitude, forgiveness and healing. The humankind is longing for peace and prosperity and not violence and bullying. No one can justify the cost of military versus the cost of human development. God has entrusted the creation to humankind but also entrusted leaders to lead nations and communities towards human development. When these powers are used inversely to its intended purpose, disaster ensue.

These powers have to be nations guarded with jealousy and strong conviction. But the most power is in the unity of nations to pursue a unified development agenda. If we look at the power that exploit, we can find the power that reconstruct.

Why are nations destroying each other? political houses tearing each other? plots against political heads being on the rise? Look at the many assassinations on flying jets. Why the rise of injustice instead of justice? It is because of an endless lust of power.

What we see in the world is not far from what is happening in our individual selves. The wanting power to control our own spaces. The desires to be better than others at the expense of many around us. Before we know it, we have eliminated the love surrounding us. The love of many people we are given to live in solidarity with. We run rage races and must win at all cost. Even if it means killing the souls of those surrounding us. Not realising that their surroundings are not just there, but there to support us in our journey of life. We are constantly concerned with appreciation, popularity, rewards, and running faster than others. We create our surroundings as rivals and concerns ourselves with influence over them.

What is happening around ourselves is comparatively what is happening in the Middle East, Asia, Sudan..... When we trace any form of threat, we strike with any form of security regardless of many thousands that will be left lying on the ground. These forms of strikes are anything to the form of a friend of influence, surveillance, military strikes, eliminations.

A form of insecurity that is destructive, giving us a sense of who we are and what we do.

Wherever we use power to give us a sense of ourselves, we separate ourselves from the rest and become diabolic. This is so applicable also to our economic and political power. The most dangerous power is the power used incorrectly in the name of serving the people. Millions of people are hurt by hopeless hope of promise. A promise to upliftment, liberation, peace and stability, access to economic activity, reduction of sickness. When these remain visible in the eyes of many day by day, hope for a better life dies.

> The most dangerous
> power is the power
> used incorrectly in
> the name of serving
> the people

Thousands of men and women goes astray and find ways to control their environments. They turn away from their governments because they experience the expression of power when they are expecting the expression of liberation.

The devastating influence of power in the hands of elected leaders become very clear when we think of the policies of apartheid until these very days. These powers create the fertile soil for societal divisions and despair.

The colossuses against apartheid saw through the power of apartheid and were bestowed with power to dismantle it. They fought a good fight to bring the divided human race to unity. Much as this fight is not completely won, it has made mountain strides. Pockets of derogatory remarks are still visible in some against the human race. While physical markings of segregation have been removed in common areas, segregation still occurs silently loud in economic spaces.

It was through the power of suffering that the power of apartheid was removed. The power of continuing suffering, poverty, inequality and economic suppression is the power to total emancipation of the human race. This is not a fight that is going to be won over the barrel of a gun, but a fight that is going to be won through the power of longing and thirst. It is a guaranteed victory because no one or whoever can stop this mighty power. It is not far from happening, it is close. No one can stop this fire.

Total power assumption will be a total liberation of a human race. This power is key, but upon acquiring, it must be used with wisdom to the benefit of the nation. It is the power for human race liberation, not power for leaders liberation. It is the power bestowed upon the nation. It is power for unity not division and destruction.

Yes of course those who have destructive and suppression powers are fighting hard to retain their power. They are doing everything possible to collapse the coming power. They are so relentless because they have realised they are fighting a losing battle. They resort to all sort of power containment tactics.

They install divisions, conflict, confusion and most importantly centralising the economic base. Their fear has collapsed them already, yet they still want to appear brave.

Stay focused on what is necessary and do not allow attention to be divided by many distractions. The nation is called to deepen its bond of friendship and love. A corner stone to success to this mission.

Our world is ruled by diabolic powers that divide and destroy. Does being weak in suffering mean we should be passive to our course? does it mean we should be soft and allow the powers of suppression to dominate us? Does it mean the economic weakness, physical and emotional weaknesses have now suddenly become virtues? Does it mean that people must now brag about their poverty as a blessing that calls for gratitude? The liberation power calls us to be true vanguards of the power that heals the wounds of humanity and renews the face of the earth.

Yes, we are poor, gentle, warming, hungry and thirsty for justice. Most of all pure of heart, peace makers who are always persecuted by a hostile world. But we are no weak links. The earth is our inheritance. The dismantling of evil economic powers is our call. It is this power that gives birth to leaders of our communities. Women and men who are strong, brave and wise to take risk and new initiatives.

This power bestows courage that enables us to deal with our oppressors. To talk straight and without hesitation about sharing wealth with those who illegally accumulated it.

We will never be free until all nations are free. We will not escape the bondage of the world hostilities until all nations become friendly amongst each other. We will never prosper until all inhabitants of the land can equally benefit from the creation

But realising success to this course we have to realise that winning is not something we are merely given in life, it is something we have to take. It needs patriots with zeal of eager to climb the mountain. We have to unleash our strength and optimism to be able to carry on and reach the tip of the mountain. This is the power in us. The power to make good judgements and choices. The power to pull each other up, and not leave one another behind.

The power to manoeuvre the adversities ahead of us. Of course, there are challenges and will ever be in this journey. But the power to outsmart them is so much of a firebrand than to give up along the way. The road to rightful skilling and empowering cannot be underestimated. While this power is exercised, we should avoid the mistakes of the past powers. The powers of destruction and division.

We will never be free until all nations are free. We will not escape the bondage of the world hostilities until all nations become friendly amongst each other. We will never prosper until all inhabitants of the land can equally benefit from the creation. If not, we will find ourselves being slaves of safeguarding our security against possible threats instead of multiplying the fruits of our inheritance.

There is no better way to life than to take your rightful position in humanity. It is a great choice to pick. A choice that will put smiles to billions of the next generations after us. Imagine the power of political freedom, economic freedom and spiritual freedom coupled together.

Imagine nations living side by side in peace and harmony, sharing the creation and its resources for the equal benefit of each other. The power to transform the economic course is a calling and is bestowed upon us. It is a path to total liberation and total justice for all human race. The evil gains of white monopoly capital and foreign domination must be conquered at all cost. Because we are born free, therefore we should live in freedom and not be chained by man-made greed and lust for destructive power. We must be aware of our limitations as to be able to use our strengths in the best possible way. The power of self-realisation.

"If you want to go faster go alone, If you want to go far go together"
African Proverb

"Our deepest fear is not that we are

inadequate.

Our Deepest fear is that we are

powerful"

- Nelson Mandela

Peace is costly but it is worth the
expense.

~Kenyan proverb

Milk and honey have different colours,
but they share the same house
peacefully.

~ African proverb

He who is destined for power does not
have to fight for it.
~ Ugandan proverb

Two ants do not fail to pull one
grasshopper.

~ Tanzanian proverb

A united family eats from the same plate.

~ Baganda proverb

Brothers love each other when they are equally rich.

~ African proverb

Poverty is slavery.

~Somalia

"We do not want to be reminded that it is we, the indigenous people, who are poor and exploited in the land of our birth."

- Steve Biko

"As long as poverty, injustice and gross inequality persist in our world, none of us can truly rest"

- Nelson Mandela

Africa

Legend:
- Oil
- Food / Drink
- Metals / Minerals
- Precious Metals / Minerals
- Wood Products
- Textile / Apparel
- Machinery / Transportation
- Electronics Related
- Other

Source: CIA Factbook
Simran Khosla/ GlobalPost

Map labels:
Clothing & Textiles, Petroleum & Natural Gas, Crude Oil, Crude Oil & Petroleum Products, Clothing & Textiles, Phosphates, Iron Ore, Cotton, Uranium, Oil, Gold, Livestock, Coffee (in Husk), Fish, Peanut Products, Fish, Aluminum, Gold, Coffee, Diamonds, Cocoa Beans, Oil, Cotton, Petroleum & Petroleum Products, Crude Oil, Diamonds, Grains, Coffee, Livestock, Timber, Crude Oil, Diamonds, Coffee, Tea, Petroleum, Gold, Crude Oil, Copper, Tobacco, Aluminum, Diamonds, Platinum, Coffee, Gold, Diamonds, Soft Drink Concentrates, Clothing & Shoes

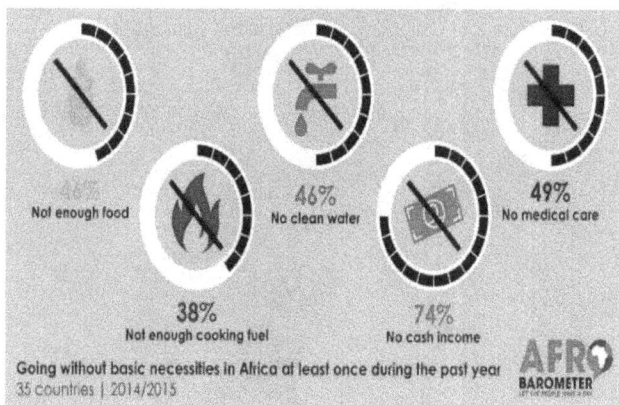

46%
Not enough food

46%
No clean water

49%
No medical care

38%
Not enough cooking fuel

74%
No cash income

Going without basic necessities in Africa at least once during the past year
35 countries | 2014/2015

AFRO
BAROMETER

Apartheid and the People of South Africa		
	Blacks	*Whites*
Population	19 million	4.5 million
Land Allocation	13 percent	87 percent
Share of National Income	< 20 percent	75 percent
Ratio of average earnings	1	14
Minimum taxable income	360 rands	750 rands
Doctors/population	1/44,000	1/400
Infant mortality rate	20% (urban)	2.7%
	40% (rural)	
Annual expenditure on education per pupil	$45	$696
Teacher/pupil ratio	1/60	1/22

Figure 1: Disproportionate Treatment circa 1978. Source: [Leo80]